IN

the

REVIVAL

GOOD NEWS & CHANGED HEARTS SINCE 9/11

JOEL C. ROSENBERG

Tyndale House Publishers, Inc.
Carol Stream, Illinois

Visit Tyndale's exciting Web site at www.tyndale.com.

TYNDALE and Tyndale's quill logo are registered trademarks
of Tyndale House Publishers, Inc.

Inside the Revival: Good News & Changed Hearts Since 9/11

This booklet is adapted from *Inside the Revolution* copyright © 2009
by Joel C. Rosenberg. All rights reserved.

Designed by Dean H. Renninger

ISBN 978-1-4143-3800-2

Printed in the United States of America

16   15   14   13   12   11   10
 7   6   5   4   3   2   1

CONTENTS

THE BIG,
UNTOLD STORY

*The greatest spiritual awakening in the
history of the Middle East is under way.*

You RARELY HEAR about it on the news.

You rarely even hear about it in churches in the West, in the East, or even in the Middle East. But the big, untold story is that more Muslims are coming to faith in Jesus Christ today than at any other time in history.

For many Muslims, despair and despondency at what they see as the utter failure of Islamic governments and societies to improve their lives and give them peace, security, and a sense of purpose and meaning in life are causing them to leave Islam in search of truth. Some have lost their way entirely and become agnostics and atheists. Others have sadly turned to alcohol and drug abuse. But millions are finding that only Jesus Christ heals the ache in their hearts and the deep wounds in their souls.

For other Muslims, it is not depression but rage that is driving them away from the Qur'an and the mosque. They are seeing far too many Muslim leaders and governments and preachers both advocating and acting out cruelty toward women and children and violence even against fellow Muslims.

And as their anger has risen, so too has their determination to disassociate themselves with Islam and find the truth someplace else.

In my travels through the epicenter I have personally witnessed—and been blessed by—God's love for Muslims and for nominal Christians. He is reviving them both. He is awaking Muslims to the truth of the Scriptures, and Muslim Background Believers ("MBBs") are finding hope in Jesus Christ. He is also breathing new spiritual life into Nominal Christian Background Believers ("NCBBs"), who were raised in churches but were long unaware of the life-changing power of Jesus Christ.

And He is doing so in numbers few could ever have imagined.

REVIVAL IN IRAN

"If you are working in Iran, you feel like you are working with God," a top Iranian ministry leader told me. "He is with us in Iran. Jesus Christ is revealing Himself to people in Iran. A big revival is under way and more is coming. Friends keep telling me to leave the country for my own safety. 'The government will arrest you,' they say. 'They will kill you.' But if you leave, you are losing a big, historical chance. If you stay and serve, you will see a big revival and see prophecy fulfilled. You feel so small. But God is so big!"[1]

At the time of the Islamic Revolution in 1979, there were only about five hundred known Muslim converts to Jesus inside the country. By 2000, a survey of Christian demographic trends reported that there were two hundred twenty thousand Christians inside Iran, of which between four and twenty thousand were Muslim converts.[2] And according to Iranian Christian leaders I interviewed, the number of Christ followers inside their country shot dramatically higher between 2000 and 2008.

"In Iran," one Iranian Christian told me, "you don't go after people with the gospel. They are coming to you to ask you about the Lord. Let me give you an example. I went to the doctor's office because I was feeling very ill. I asked the receptionist if I could see the doctor right away, but she was a veiled woman and a fanatical Muslim. She had no intention of making life easier for an 'infidel,' and she told me I would have to wait for two hours. 'You will regret that,' I said with a smile, and then sat down in the crowded waiting room. A few moments later, the doctor walked by to pick up a file. 'Hello, Reverend,' he said to me. I greeted him back. Then everyone in the waiting room asked me, 'Are you really a reverend?' I said I was. 'How can I know Jesus?' they asked. I told them and five Muslims prayed with me in the waiting room to receive Christ as their Savior. 'See how you will regret making me wait?' I told the receptionist, again with a smile. She has never made me wait again."[3]

Ultimately, I'm told that what is bringing these Iranians to Christ are dreams and visions of Jesus himself. Several years ago, an Iranian pastor I know met a twenty-two-year-old Iranian Shia woman who had become a Christian after seeing a vision of Jesus Christ. She just showed up in his church one day, hungry to study the Bible for herself. The more she studied God's Word, the more deeply she loved Jesus. Soon, she discovered that God had given her the spiritual gift of evangelism. That is, not only did she have a passion to share her faith with others; the Holy Spirit had also blessed her with a supernatural ability to lead Muslims to Jesus. Today, she leads an average of fifteen people to Christ every day— that's right, *fifteen a day*. She told my pastor friend that Iranian Muslims are so desperate for the gospel that typically it takes about five minutes to share the story of her conversion and how God has changed her life before the listener is ready to also receive Christ. "Difficult" conversations, she says, with several questions or concerns, take fifteen to twenty minutes. Her prayer: to lead seven thousand Iranian Muslims to Christ over the next five years.[4]

REVIVAL IN AFRICA

Senior pastors and ministry leaders in Egypt estimate there are more than 2.5 million followers of Jesus Christ in their country. Many of these are Muslim converts, and there is also an enormous revival going on among nominal Christians inside the historic Coptic church, whose members number about 10 million.[5]

On a trip to Cairo, I visited the famous "garbage church" planted in 1978 by a Coptic priest with a burden for reaching the people who lived among literally thousands of tons of trash—people Paul called "the scum of the world, the dregs of all things"*—to share the Good News that they could be adopted by the King of kings. Now, on an average weekend, some ten thousand new and growing believers from the garbage community come to worship and grow as disciples of Jesus Christ.

In Sudan, meanwhile, one of the biggest stories in modern Christendom is unfolding—a spiritual awakening of almost unimaginable proportions amid civil war, radical Islam, rampant persecution, and outright genocide.

In *Epicenter*, I reported that one million Sudanese had turned to Christ since the year 2000—not in spite of persecution, war, and genocide, but *because* of them. "People see what radical Islam is like," one Sudanese Christian leader told me, "and they want Jesus instead."[6]

Since the fall of 2006, more than a quarter of a million additional Sudanese have given their lives to Christ, bringing the estimated total number of believers in the country to more than 5.5 million.[7]

The number of believers in Libya is not currently known. In Tunisia, I am told, there are less than a thousand Muslim Background Believers

---

* I Corinthians 4:13.

("MBBs"). But in neighboring Algeria, more than eighty thousand Muslims have become followers of Christ in recent years. The vast majority of these believers are young people under the age of thirty.[8]

The surge of Christianity has become so alarming to Islamic clerics that in March of 2006, Algerian officials passed a law banning Muslims from becoming Christians or even learning about Christianity, and forbidding Christians from meeting together without a license from the government.[9]

On a 2005 trip to Casablanca and Rabat, I found the Moroccan media up in arms about the "phenomenon of Moroccans converting to Christianity," suggesting that between 20,000 and 40,000 Muslims have become Christ-followers. Local pastors and ministry leaders have told me that the kinds of numbers cited in these stories may be overstated, but they readily acknowledge that God is on the move in their country. Many MBBs are now evangelists, disciple makers, and church planters overflowing with exciting stories of how other Moroccans are coming to Christ. Let me share just one with you.

A young Muslim woman from Morocco—let's call her Abidah (which means "worshiper")—saw the *JESUS* film while living and working in Europe and became a follower of Jesus. After two years of being discipled in the faith by an older and wiser believer, Abidah went home on vacation to visit her family in Morocco. For five days she prayed about how to tell her family that she had become a Christian, but she was too scared. On the sixth day, her sister also returned home from Europe. "Hey, look what I got for free!" the sister said to her family, showing them a copy of the Injil (New Testament) and the *JESUS* film a Christian had given her as a gift on the ferry ride across the Mediterranean.

"Hey, look, the film is about Isa!"* exclaimed the father, a traditional Muslim. "He's our prophet. Let's all watch it."

Abidah was in shock.

The family sat down together in front of the television. About halfway through the film, the whole family was asking one question after another, trying to understand who Jesus was, why He taught the way He did, and how He could do miracles and show such love and compassion to everyone, including His enemies.

Abidah saw her opening. She started answering the questions. Now it was her family who was in shock. "Why do you know all these things?" asked her father.

---

* Isa is the Arabic name for Jesus.

"Because I saw this movie two years ago and I became a Christian. But I've been afraid to tell you."

A cloud covered her father's face. He looked angry. But when he spoke, he did not yell at Abidah. Instead, he said, "What! You made us wait five days to hear about Jesus?"

REVIVAL IN IRAQ

Without a doubt, the hunger for Christ inside Iraq is also at an all-time high, say the numerous Iraqi pastors and ministry leaders I interviewed. Several million Arabic New Testaments and Christian books have been shipped into Iraq since the liberation. Millions more are being printed inside the country, and pastors say they cannot keep up with the demand. What's more, Iraqis today are turning to Christ in numbers unimaginable at any point during Saddam Hussein's reign of terror.

Before 2003, senior Iraqi Christian leaders tell me, there were only about four to six hundred known born-again followers of Jesus Christ in the entire country, despite an estimated seven hundred fifty thousand nominal Christians in historic Iraqi churches. By the end of 2008, Iraqi Christian leaders estimated that there were more than seventy thousand born-again Iraqi believers.[10]

Why such spiritual hunger? Every Iraqi Christian I have interviewed has given me the same two answers: war and persecution. Though the security in Iraq was deteriorating from 2003 to 2007, one of the top leaders of the Revivalist movement there told me he had never seen so many Iraqis praying to receive Christ and wanting Bible teaching.

I asked him how he accounted for such developments.

"It's not that complicated really, Joel," he replied. "When human beings are under threat, they look for a strong power to help them—a refuge. Iraqis look around and when they see believers in Jesus enjoying internal peace during a time of such violence and fear, they want Jesus too."[11]

REVIVAL IN THE HOLY LAND

In the heart of the epicenter itself—Jerusalem, Judea, Samaria, and Gaza—signs of revival are finally noticeable after centuries of spiritual drought.

Just since 2007, nearly one thousand Muslims have come to Christ in the West Bank alone, most of them converted through dreams and visions of Jesus.

One of the most influential Revivalists I have ever met is a Palestinian Arab. Born to a nominal

Christian family in Jerusalem in 1947, Taheer was barely six months old when the first Arab-Israeli war broke out. His mother died soon thereafter. Nevertheless, God was incredibly gracious to him, bringing him to saving faith in Jesus Christ at the age of eighteen as he wept on his knees with repentance after finally reading the New Testament for himself.

"I will not leave you as orphans," Jesus said in John 14:18-19. "I will come to you. After a little while the world will no longer see Me, but you will see Me; because I live, you will live also." These verses were suddenly coming true in this man's life, and he soon developed a passion for reaching Muslims and nominal Christians with God's amazing grace.

REVIVAL IN SYRIA, LEBANON, AND JORDAN

In 1967, there were no known born-again followers of Jesus Christ from a Muslim background in the entire country of Syria. Today, there are between four and five thousand born-again believers in the country, both MBBs and NCBBs combined.

Does more need to be done? Absolutely. But as one Arab ministry leader there told me: "I am so excited because God is doing a miracle in Syria."

God has been reviving the Jordanian Church in

the last four decades, and particularly in the past few years. Conservative estimates say the number of believers in the country is now between five and ten thousand. The head of one major Jordanian ministry, however, believes there may be as many as fifty thousand believers in the country.[12] Again, the precise numbers are not as important as the trend, and the Church is definitely bearing fruit again after centuries of spiritual barrenness.

In Lebanon, sources tell me, there are about ten thousand truly born-again followers of Jesus Christ today, though nearly four in ten of the country's 4 million residents describe themselves as "Christian." Most of the believers are NCBBs, but Muslims are staring to show an openness to the gospel that has been lacking for centuries.

As the Second Lebanon War erupted in July of 2006, Lebanese Revivalists huddled together to fast and pray for their country, even as rockets and bombs were falling all around them and the mood of the people was quickly darkening.

The believers soon found themselves drawn to Matthew 5:14-16, in which Jesus said, "You are the light of the world. A city set on a hill cannot be hidden; nor does anyone light a lamp and put it under a basket, but on the lampstand, and it gives light to all who are in the house. Let your light shine before men in such a way that they may see your good works, and glorify your Father who is in heaven."

They decided they needed to spring into action, not wait for the war to be over. They mobilized dozens of teams to begin doing relief work among the Shia families from southern Lebanon who had fled to the Beirut area for safety. In just a few short weeks, with financial help from the Joshua Fund, they delivered forty thousand packages of food, cooking supplies, New Testaments, and the *JESUS* film on DVD to these displaced and terrified families. They also drove trucks filled with relief supplies and gospel literature to Shia families hunkered down in the south as well as those in the Bekaa Valley, near the border with Syria.

"Food they need, but Jesus they need more," said an Arab Christian ministry worker. Through that outreach alone, more than 1,100 Lebanese Muslims prayed to receive Christ as their Savior.

REVIVAL IN SAUDI ARABIA

In Saudi Arabia—the epicenter of Islam due to its status as the home of Mecca and Medina—a dramatic spiritual awakening is taking place. Arab Christian leaders estimated there were more than one hundred thousand Saudi MBBs in 2005, and they believe the numbers are even higher today.

Consider one example. A Saudi woman—let's call her Marzuqah (which means "blessed by God")—secretly converted to Christianity. But she had a brother who was dying of a terrible disease, and Marzuqah was deeply grieved. She prayed fervently for God to heal and to save her brother.

One day, Jesus appeared to Marzuqah in a dream. "Your prayers have been answered," He told her. "Go tell your brother about Me." She did.

To her astonishment, her brother prayed with her to receive Christ. Though the rest of her family has not yet followed her lead, Marzuqah has become a devoted disciple. She studies her Bible two hours a day. She has found other secret believers to meet with for prayer and Bible study. And she is sharing the gospel with her Muslim friends. "There are so many people I must tell about Jesus!" she says.[13]

REVIVAL IN CENTRAL ASIA

Is God moving powerfully in Afghanistan? He most certainly is. Some sources told me the number of Afghan believers is now between 20,000 and 30,000. That could be true, but I honestly did not see evidence that there are even 10,000 at present, and persecution of the believers is intense.

The enormous controversy over the case of Abdul Rahman, a Muslim convert to Christianity facing execution by a court in Kabul for apostasy, shone a huge spotlight on the fact that Afghans are turning to Christ in such numbers that Islamic leaders are furious. It also showed the fledgling Afghan church that fellow believers around the world are praying for them and eager to see them grow and flourish.

Evangelical leaders in Kazakhstan report that there are more than fifteen thousand Kazakh Christians, and more than one hundred thousand Christians of all ethnicities, and the stories I hear from Kazakhstan today are extraordinary.

During the summer of 1986, I had the privilege of traveling to Tashkent, the capital of Uzbekistan. At the time, there were only a few Uzbek believers in a country of 27 million people. Today, there are some thirty thousand Uzbek followers of Christ, and hunger for the gospel is at an all-time high.

Senior Pakistani Christian leaders tell me there is a "conversion explosion" going on in their country. There are now an estimated 2.5 million to 3 million born-again Pakistani believers worshiping Jesus

Christ. Whole towns and villages along the Afghan-Pakistani border are seeing dreams and visions of Jesus and are converting to Christianity.

One young Pakistani Muslim who converted to Christianity became a bold minister of the gospel to Taliban refugees. Over the course of two to three years, the thirty-one-year-old evangelist personally led eight hundred Taliban extremists to faith in Christ before he was captured and murdered and his car set ablaze by a bloodthirsty mob.

My friend Dr. T. E. Koshy, a senior elder in one of India's largest evangelical church-planting movements, began traveling to Pakistan in 1993 to preach the gospel and strengthen the local believers. "Today, with so many Christians in Pakistan, many are seeing the believers demonstrate Christ's love in real and practical ways," he said. "The restlessness of the masses is created by the Enemy, and Pakistanis are coming to realize that they can only find rest and healing and forgiveness through Jesus Christ."

AIR WAR, GROUND WAR

How followers of Jesus are reaching Muslims with the gospel

IN THE PAGES AHEAD, I will profile some of the most effective tactics I have encountered among Revivalists in the Middle East. But first, let me be clear about an extremely important point. I use the imagery of "air war" and "ground war," but I do not mean to suggest that the followers of Christ would ever resort to military weapons to force their beliefs on others. To the contrary, the Bible teaches them to wage *only* a spiritual war, a war of ideas and beliefs, not a physical war.

These Revivalists argue with great conviction that biblical Christianity is not a Western, colonialist, or imperialist religion. Nor is it some foreign ideology imposed on the Muslim world to enslave or hinder it. Rather, Revivalists assert that biblical Christianity is a movement that was born in the Middle East, a spiritually and personally liberating force, the most powerful liberating force in human history. They believe that a personal relationship with God through faith in Jesus Christ changes hearts so that the violent become men and women of peace and reconciliation. And they believe this not because someone told them about it but because they have experienced it for themselves.

Thus, they thank God every morning for a new day and for continued life. Then they pray that God would fill them with the Holy Spirit, suit them up in the full armor of God, give them the strength and the courage to do and say whatever He commands them, and accomplish His divine purposes for that day in and through their lives.

THE "AIR WAR"

Radio is one powerful weapon in the evangelical air war. Trans World Radio, for example, broadcasts biblical programming in Arabic for twenty-eight hours a week, targeting the Middle East and North Africa. They receive more than two hundred thousand letters a year from listeners seeking answers, requesting

Arabic Bibles, requesting Bible correspondence courses, and sharing their stories of how they came to faith by listening to TWR's programs. Other radio ministries have similar approaches and results.

Today, satellite television has become another breakthrough strategy to advance the gospel in the Muslim world. And what is amazing to me is just how many people in the epicenter have satellite dishes, even if they own almost no other material possessions.

Today there are no fewer than sixteen different Christian television channels operating on the "Hot Bird" satellites run by the European telecommunications company Eutelsat.* One Christian network known as SAT-7 is regularly seen by at least 9 million viewers throughout North Africa and the Middle East.

You have probably never heard of Father Zakaria Botros. But you need to know his story. He is far and away the most watched and most effective Arab evangelist operating in the Muslim world, and he is by far the most controversial. His

---

* Christian channels in the epicenter include: Al Hayat; SAT-7 in Arabic, Persian, Turkish, and North African dialects; Miracle TV; Three Angels Broadcasting Network; the God Channel; the Spirit Channel; Smile (a Christian channel for children in the Middle East); and five networks run by the Trinity Broadcasting Network.

enemies do not simply want to silence him. They want to assassinate him. An Arabic newspaper has named Botros "Islam's Public Enemy #1."[1]

Why are Radical Muslims so enraged by a Coptic priest from Egypt who is in his seventies? Because Botros is waging an air war against them, and he is winning.

His ninety-minute program—a combination of preaching, teaching, and answering questions from (often irate) callers all over the world—has become "must-see TV" throughout the Muslim world—viewed by an estimated 50 million Muslims a day. Botros pulls no punches on the air or off. He tells Muslims what he believes is wrong with their religion, no matter how painful it may be to hear. But he also believes passionately that God loves the whole world, including each and every Muslim. He believes that *whoever* believes in the lordship of Jesus Christ—Jew, Muslim, or otherwise—will, in fact, receive eternal life.

"I believe this is the hand of God," Botros told me when we spoke by phone in September 2008. "He is directing me. He shows me what to say. He shows me what to write on the Web sites. He is showing me more and more how to use technology to reach people with his message of redemption."

I consider my friend Hormoz Shariat to be the Billy Graham of Iran. He is without question the most recognizable and most influential Iranian evangelist in the world. Every night in prime time, Shariat broadcasts by satellite a live program in which he shares the gospel in his native Farsi, teaches in-depth Bible studies, and takes phone calls from Muslims who have sincere questions or simply want to attack him on the air. And given that he is hosting a program unlike anything on Iranian state-run television, Shariat draws an enormous audience, an estimated 7 to 9 million Iranians every night.

Most remarkable to me is that Shariat did not grow up hoping to be an evangelist. In 1979, he and his wife were actually part of the Iranian Revolution.

Shariat told me, "Joel, I'm often asked, 'What does Christianity have to offer Muslims?' I can only report from my own experience and from personally witnessing the effects on thousands of others that have come to Christ from Islam through our ministry. By far, the most expressed benefits are peace and joy—which are direct results of salvation. As Jesus says in John 14:27, 'Peace I leave with you; My peace I give to you; not as the world gives do I give to you. Do not let your heart be troubled, nor let it be fearful.'

"Muslims do not enjoy the assurance of salvation. I have heard the prayers of devout Muslims begging God to deliver them from torture in the grave and the fires of hell. Unlike Muslims, Christians have the assurance of salvation. After all, the Bible tells us that salvation is a free gift of God's grace. It is not something we can earn. It is not something we can buy. It is something God gives us for free. All we have to do is accept it. Acts 16:31 says 'Believe in the Lord Jesus Christ, and you will be saved.' Romans 6:23 says, 'For the wages of sin is death, but the free gift of God is eternal life in Christ Jesus our Lord.' 1 John 5:13 says, 'These things I have written to you who believe in the name of the Son of God, so that you may *know* that you have eternal life.' Christians can really know beyond the shadow of a doubt that we are saved and going to heaven. Muslims cannot.

"When I accepted Christ as my Savior, Joel, my heart was filled with peace and joy. It was the most extraordinary thing. And now, one of the greatest rewards of my ministry is to hear Iranian Muslims tell me that they, too, are experiencing peace and joy because they have accepted Jesus Christ as their personal Savior and have come to understand His assurance of salvation."[2]

"BOOTS ON THE GROUND"

Revivalists are deeply grateful to the Lord for providing radio, satellite television, and increasingly the Internet as powerful and effective new ways of reaching vast numbers of Muslims with the gospel and biblical precepts.

But ultimately, the Revivalists say, their hope for transforming the Muslim world is not in technology but in human beings who have been "revived"—spiritually transformed by faith in Jesus Christ and filled with the power of the Holy Spirit of God.

The key is the personal touch. The Muslim culture is an Eastern culture, not a Western one. It is based on relationships and storytelling and on people spending long periods of time with one another. People in Eastern cultures are not so worried about schedules and quotas and sales figures and returning e-mails and phone calls quickly. They are interested in personal contact. They are interested in firm handshakes and good food and strong coffee and sweet tea and looking in a man's eyes to see if he is a good man or a bad man and whether he can be trusted or not.

In such a culture, a spiritual revolution cannot all be waged or won by remote control. It cannot all be done from radio and TV studios in Europe or the U.S., or via e-mail and Web sites. Some of it—much of it—must be done face-to-face, person-to-person. The Revivalists say there is no other way.

Can that be dangerous? Absolutely. Hamid is one of the most wanted Iranian Revivalists in the world.[*] Precisely because he is so effective in recruiting and training Iranian evangelists, disciple makers, pastors, and church planters, the Iranian secret police have hunted him for years. They nearly assassinated him in 1994, but by God's grace he and his family narrowly escaped with their lives.

"The turning point," he told me, "happened in 1974. I had already graduated from college. I was a mechanical engineer, and I was working for an oil company. But one day I met a Christian leader from Pakistan who was traveling through Iran looking for someone to start a nationwide ministry in that country." Hamid said he had little interest in helping the Pakistani.

"Three months later, the Pakistani returned to Iran and invited me to attend a conference outside

---

[*] Hamid is not his real name; it is a pseudonym to protect this Iranian Christian leader. For security reasons, I cannot disclose when or where I interviewed him, but I can say it was within the last two years.

the country about evangelism and discipleship," Hamid said. "I was curious, so I agreed to go. While I was there, a voice in my heart asked me, 'What do you want to do with the rest of your life?' I wasn't sure. I liked working for the oil company. But the voice said to me, 'Every day, thousands are going to hell.'

"For three days and nights I struggled with God. Finally I knew what I had to do. I went back to Tehran and resigned from the oil company. The Pakistani arranged for me to receive nine months of ministry training. Then in 1975, I started a ministry to reach all of Iran with the gospel.

"We concentrated on five things from the beginning," he said. "First, we identified men and women from many churches who displayed a passion for the Lord, and we asked them if they would like us to disciple them. Second, we took our disciples to parks to practice witnessing [telling people about their faith in Christ]. Third, we recruited and trained four disciples to become full-time staff members with our ministry, because we knew we couldn't do it on our own, and we didn't want to do it alone. Fourth, we started a Bible school by correspondence. Fifth, we held conferences and special meetings."

Because of his high profile, Hamid is now in

exile. He misses his country, and he misses his friends. But he has no regrets. He said he believes God is using him far more now that he is living on the outside where he can study and teach and preach and travel freely without fear of arrest, or worse.

"Just look what God is doing in Iran today," he said. "How can I not be grateful to the Lord? I wouldn't have believed in 1974 that we could see millions of believers in Iran. . . . Now, there are too many calls coming into our offices from people who have accepted Christ or want to know more about Jesus. We don't have time to answer them all."

And that, Hamid says, is why he focuses on training leaders capable of responding to the spiritual revolution Jesus has unleashed in Iran. "Like Jesus said, 'The harvest is plentiful, but the laborers are few; therefore beseech the Lord of the harvest to send out laborers into His harvest.'"*

---

* Luke 10:2

"ISLAM IS NOT THE ANSWER, AND JIHAD IS NOT THE WAY; JESUS IS THE WAY"

The theology of the Revivalists—
Who are they, and what do they want?

TASS SAADA was a killer.

He and his friends murdered Jews in Israel. They murdered civilians and soldiers alike. They attacked Christians in Jordan. Sometimes they tossed hand grenades at Christians' homes. Other times they strafed houses with machine-gun fire. They once tried to assassinate the crown prince of an Arab country. They nearly succeeded. And they did all this willingly. They did it eagerly. Saada certainly did. His nickname was once *Jazzar*— "butcher." It was a moniker he relished.

Saada was not expecting to become a follower of Jesus Christ.

"I was a Palestinian sniper," Saada would later tell me. "But then I fell in love with a Savior who loves Arabs as well as Jews."

In his remarkable book, *Once an Arafat Man*, Saada explained his realization that the God of the Bible loves us all with an unfathomable, everlasting, unquenchable love. He explained that God's love is so amazing, so divine, that He actually offers all of us—Jew and Gentile alike—the free gift of salvation through the death and resurrection of His Son, Jesus Christ.

Tass Saada is no longer a Radical—he is a Revivalist. He no longer believes that Islam is the answer. He no longer believes jihad is the way. He believes that Jesus is the Way, the Truth, and the Life and that no one can have a personal relationship with God without accepting that Jesus is the Messiah, just as the Bible teaches in John 14:6.

The Revivalists say that what happened in the early church two thousand years ago is happening again today. They say that because Jesus is God, He has all power. He is the King of kings and the

Lord of lords. Thus, when He gives His disciples an order, it must be followed. And that order, they note, is to preach the gospel to the whole world and make disciples—not just "Christians" but truly dedicated and devoted Christ-followers—of "all the nations."

Not just the safe nations.

Not just the democratic nations.

Not just the free market nations.

Jesus told His disciples to go make more disciples in *all* the nations.

Even the difficult nations.

Even the dangerous nations.

Even the Radical nations.

Reaching the entire world—and particularly the world of Islam—with the gospel is an enormously challenging mission. Many Revivalists readily concede that, humanly speaking, they feel overwhelmed by the task. But they are commanded to be *living* sacrifices—people devoting their very lives to serve and to save the lives of others.

WHAT THEY BELIEVE, VERSE BY VERSE

After spending time with dozens of ministry leaders throughout the epicenter, I have concluded that while Revivalists hold many important theological beliefs, they have at least five common core theological convictions based on their steadfast belief that the Bible is the holy Word of God.

These are not unique convictions. Indeed, they are shared by fully devoted followers of Jesus Christ all over the world. Nevertheless it is both important and remarkable that former Muslims—not a few of whom are former Radicals—hold such convictions.

Core Conviction No. 1: God Loves All of Mankind

Each and every one of the Revivalists I interviewed noted with deep conviction that according to the Bible, God's defining character trait is love. The Bible teaches that God loves every man, woman, and child on the face of the earth—regardless of race, nationality, tribe, or language.

God loves all of us with an everlasting love. He loved all of us before we loved Him. He loves us so much that He wants to adopt us into His family as His children and let us live with Him in heaven forever. He loves us so much that if we let Him, He will be a Shepherd to us, guiding us, providing for us, protecting us, giving us rest, and taking care of us in every possible way. He loves us so much that if we follow and obey Him, we can actually become friends with Him and develop a personal, intimate relationship with Him.

Here are some of the verses the Revivalists point to in describing the love of this incredible God:

"God is love." —*1 John 4:16*

"For God so loved the world, that He gave His only begotten Son, that whoever believes in Him shall not perish, but have eternal life." —*John 3:16*

"I have loved you with an everlasting love; therefore I have drawn you with loving-kindness." —*Jeremiah 31:3*

"Give thanks to the Lord, for He is good, for His lovingkindness is everlasting. Give thanks to the God of gods, for his loving-kindness is everlasting. Give thanks to the Lord of lords, for his lovingkindness is everlasting." —*Psalm 136:1-3*

[Jesus said,] "You are My friends if you do what I command you. No longer do I call you slaves, for the slave does not know what his master is doing; but I have called you friends, for all things that I have heard from My Father I have made known to you." —*John 15:14-15*

"Do not envy a man of violence and do not
choose any of his ways. For the devious
are an abomination to the Lord; but He
is intimate with the upright."
—*Proverbs 3:31-32*

The Revivalists note with equal conviction that
the Bible also teaches that because God loves all
mankind, He also has a wonderful plan and purpose for every man, woman, and child. Consider
these verses:

"For I know the plans I have for you," says
the Lord. "They are plans for good and
not for disaster, to give you a future and
a hope. In those days when you pray,
I will listen. If you look for me whole-
heartedly, you will find me."
—*Jeremiah 29:11-13, NLT*

[Jesus said,] "I came that they may have
life, and have it abundantly."
—*John 10:10*

"And we know that God causes all things to
work together for good to those who love
God, to those who are called according to
His purpose." —*Romans 8:28*

"God . . . desires all men to be saved and to

come to the knowledge of the truth."
—*1 Timothy 2:3-4*

"We are His workmanship, created in Christ
Jesus for good works, which God prepared
beforehand so that we would walk in
them." —*Ephesians 2:10*

Core Conviction No. 2: All Mankind Is Sinful and Thus Separated from God

Most people are not terrorists, of course. Most
of us have not been trained to kill "infidels" and
recruit others to do the same. Nevertheless, the
Bible teaches that every man, woman, and child
has sinned against God. We have either generally
disregarded Him—paying Him and His Word
scant interest or attention—or we have actively
disobeyed Him. Either way, this is sin.

The problem, the Bible makes clear, is that our
sins separate us from loving relationship with God.
Our sins also condemn us to eternal death where
we will be separated from God in hell forever.
Why? Because God is holy and we are not.

"All have sinned and fall short of the glory
of God." —*Romans 3:23*

"The Lord has looked down from heaven

upon the sons of men to see if there are
any who understand, who seek after
God. [But] they have all turned aside,
together they have become corrupt; there
is no one who does good, not even one."
—Psalm 14:2-3

"The wages of sin is death." *—Romans 6:23*

[Jesus said,] "If your foot causes you to
stumble, cut it off; it is better for you
to enter life lame, than, having your two
feet, to be cast into hell, where . . . the
fire is not quenched." *—Mark 9:45-46*

Core Conviction No. 3: Jesus Christ Is Mankind's Only Hope of Salvation

The fact that we are all sinners separated from God
now and for eternity is terrible, depressing, devastating news, of course. Fortunately, however, the Bible
teaches that God in His unending love and kindness
made a way for us to be forgiven and to be saved
from going to hell. He made a way for us to enter an
intimate and personal relationship with Him.

As one reads the New Testament, the Revivalists note, one learns that God sent Jesus to die on a
Roman cross to pay the penalty for our sins. He died
in our place, to rescue us from hell and restore us to

a right relationship with God. He not only died on the cross, the Bible teaches, but He rose from the dead, thus proving that He is the only way to God.

> "While we were still helpless, at the right time Christ died for the ungodly. . . .
>
> God demonstrates His own love toward us, in that while we were yet sinners, Christ died for us." —*Romans 5:6, 8*

> "The wages of sin is death, but the free gift of God is eternal life in Christ Jesus our Lord." —*Romans 6:23*

> "Christ died for our sins . . . He was buried . . . He was raised on the third day according to the Scriptures . . . He appeared to [Peter], then to the twelve. After that He appeared to more than five hundred." —*1 Corinthians 15:3-6*

How, then, can one know the truth? By studying the New Testament, and then earnestly asking God to make it clear what the truth is.

Consider the following promises found in the Bible:

> "'You will call upon Me and come and pray to Me, and I will listen to you. You will seek

> Me and find Me when you search for Me
> with all your heart. I will be found by you,'
> declares the Lord." —*Jeremiah 29:12-14*
>
> "Call to Me and I will answer you," [says
> the Lord,] "and I will tell you great and
> mighty things, which you do not know."
> —*Jeremiah 33:3*
>
> [Jesus said,] "Ask, and it will be given to you;
> seek, and you will find; knock, and it
> will be opened to you. For everyone who
> asks receives, and he who seeks finds, and
> to him who knocks it will be opened."
> —*Matthew 7:7-8*

Many Muslims have come to Jesus asking, and
they have received. They have sought and found.
They knocked, and the door was opened, just as
Jesus promised.

Core Conviction No. 4: A Person Must Individually Choose to Follow Jesus Christ As Personal Savior and Lord

It is not enough simply to realize the above truths.
People must individually receive Jesus Christ
as their own personal Savior and Lord, trusting
that Jesus died on the cross to pay for the sins of
humanity, believing that Jesus rose again from the

dead, thus proving Himself to be the Messiah, and choosing by faith to become a Christ follower and accept God's free gift of salvation.

"But as many as received Him [Jesus Christ], to them He gave the right to become children of God, even to those who believe in His name." —*John 1:12*

"If you confess with your mouth Jesus as Lord, and believe in your heart that God raised Him from the dead, you will be saved; for with the heart a personal believes, resulting in righteousness, and with the mouth he confesses, resulting in salvation. . . . Whoever will call on the name of the Lord will be saved. . . . Faith comes from hearing, and hearing by the word of Christ."
—*Romans 10:9-10, 13, 17*

"For by grace [unmerited favor] you have been saved through faith; and that not of yourselves, it is the gift of God; not as a result of works, so that no one may boast."
—*Ephesians 2:8-9*

"Behold, I [Jesus] stand at the door and knock; if anyone hears My voice and opens the door, I will come in to him

and will dine with him, and he with Me."
—*Revelation 3:20*

Any person who is willing to repent—turn away from their sins and from living life as they see fit— and turn around to actually follow the God of the Bible can receive Jesus Christ as Savior and Lord. Here is a suggested prayer that has been helpful to many Muslims, Jews, and others—including my parents and me—in becoming followers of Christ. The key is not so much the precise words as the attitude of your heart.

Lord Jesus, thank You for loving me. Thank You for having a wonderful plan and purpose for my life. I need You today—I know I need You to forgive me for all of my sins. Thank You for dying on the cross to pay the penalty for my sins. Thank You for rising again from the dead to prove that You are the Way, the Truth, and the Life and the only way to get to heaven. Jesus, I confess right now with my mouth that You are the King of kings and the Lord of lords. And I believe in my heart that God raised You from the dead. And now I open the door of my heart and my life right now. I receive You as my Savior and Lord. Thank You for forgiving my sins and giving me eternal life. Please change my life. Please fill me with your Holy Spirit. Please take control of my life and make me the kind of person that You want me to be, so that I can serve You and please You forever. Thank You so much. I love You, and I want to follow You. Amen.

Any person who prays that prayer with sincere faith in Jesus Christ's death and resurrection becomes part of the family of God. The Bible teaches that several wonderful things happen as a result:

1. New spiritual life. According to the words of Jesus in John chapter 3, believers have been spiritually "born again" and have been adopted into the family of God.

2. Great joy in heaven. Jesus says in Luke 15:10 that there is great rejoicing in heaven when a person becomes a follower of the living God. "I tell you," Jesus said, "there is joy in the presence of the angels of God over one sinner who repents."

3. Hope of going to heaven. According to Jesus' words in John 3:16, believers can be certain of eternal life. Those who put their trust in Him will *not* go to hell and perish eternally when they die physically. Rather, they will go to heaven and live forever with God and all those who have been adopted into His family by faith in Jesus Christ.

4. The Holy Spirit living within them. According to the words of the apostle Paul in Ephesians 1:13-14, believers' salvation has been sealed and secured forever by God's Holy Spirit now living within them.

5. Access to a supernatural sense of peace. Paul says in Philippians 4:7 that we now have access to a supernatural peace with God and internal peace of mind, regardless of whatever external circumstances come our way. "The peace of God, which surpasses all comprehension, will guard your hearts and your minds in Christ Jesus." This does not mean believers won't face times of stress, anxiety, panic, fear, even persecution. But as a child of God and a follower of Jesus Christ, we can now pray and ask our Father in heaven to give us the "peace which surpasses all comprehension"—an overwhelming sense of calm that may not even make sense—and He promises to give you such peace.

6. Access to a supernatural sense of hope. According to the words of Hebrews 6:18-19, all followers of

Jesus Christ are encouraged to "take hold of the hope set before us" and to view "this hope we have as an anchor of the soul, a hope both sure and steadfast." We no longer need to be discouraged, depressed, or despairing. God loves us and wants to care for us; and He promises never to leave or forsake us.

7. **Access to God's supernatural wisdom.** According to James 1:5, "If any of you lacks wisdom, let him ask of God, who gives to all generously and without reproach, and it will be given to him." Whenever we face situations or decisions that confuse or perplex us, we can turn to our Father in heaven and ask for help. When we do, He promises to provide us with supernatural guidance and direction.

Core Conviction No. 5: Christ Followers Are Commanded to Love Their Neighbors and Their Enemies and to Make Disciples of All Nations

Jesus practiced what He preached. He loved people whether they deserved it or not, whether they wanted His love or not, whether they said thank you or not, whether they chose to follow Him or not, whether they blessed Him or whether they cursed Him. Even in the last moments of His life on earth, while hanging on the cross—after having been beaten and mocked and tortured in the cruelest and most inhumane ways—Jesus demonstrated His love even for His worst and most violent enemies by saying, "Father, forgive them; for they do not know what they are doing" (Luke 23:34). And this is what He expects from His followers, in the Middle East and around the world.

Consider the following words of Jesus:

"You shall love your neighbor as yourself."
—*Matthew 19:19*

"You have heard that it was said, 'You shall love your neighbor and hate your enemy.' But I say to you, love your enemies and pray for those who persecute you."
—*Matthew 5:43-44*

"I say to you who hear, love your enemies, do good to those who hate you, bless those who curse you, pray for those who mistreat you. Whoever hits you on the cheek, offer him the other also; and whoever takes away your coat, do not withhold your shirt from him either. Give to everyone who asks of you, and whoever takes away what is yours, do not demand it back. Treat others the same way you want them to treat you."
—*Luke 6:27-31*

To be sure, loving one's neighbors—and particularly loving one's enemies—can be difficult if not impossible in the Muslim world, humanly speaking. But Jesus commanded that we follow His example and do it anyway. He knew that only someone supernaturally transformed—born again—by God's love and empowered by the Holy Spirit could obey such commands. Thus, when we obey these commands in the power of the Holy Spirit, we demonstrate that we are, in fact, true followers of a living and all-powerful God.

JOIN THE
REVOLUTION

Christians have the "love your enemy"
strategy all to themselves.

IN THE ISLAMIC WORLD, only the Revivalists are teaching people to show love, mercy, and compassion to those who hate and want to destroy. No one else in the Islamic world is offering forgiveness to those who have committed acts of evil against them. Only the true followers of Jesus are doing these things, because only people who have been born again and truly transformed by the Holy Spirit have the capacity to love their enemies. None of us have that ability in and of ourselves as normal human beings. So when we demonstrate Christlike love to our enemies, we show the Muslim world that we serve a different God, the

One True God, the God of love and power and forgiveness.

Imagine if more of the Church around the world were mobilized to love our neighbors and our enemies in the name of Jesus. Already, Muslims are becoming Revivalists in record numbers. What if God wants to accelerate this trend? What if He wants us to be part of that acceleration?

My wife and I and the Joshua Fund team believe that is exactly what the Lord wants, and we have dedicated ourselves to helping mobilize the Church to pursue four simple strategies: learn, pray, give, and go. Let me close, therefore, by sharing a few thoughts with those of you who want to know more about these strategies and who may already be considering joining the Revolution and aiding the Revivalists.

Strategy No. 1: Learn

> "Look among the nations! Observe! Be astonished! Wonder! Because I am doing something in your days—you would not believe if you were told."
> —Habakkuk 1:5

First and foremost, I would encourage you to study the Bible for yourself and discover God's plan and purpose for all the people of the Middle East. You will, of course, find much about the Lord's great love for the Jewish people and the nation of Israel. At the same time, a careful reading will help you discover God's tremendous love for Iraqis, Iranians, Egyptians, Kurds, Arabs, Turks, and many others in the epicenter as well. I have no doubt that the more you study the Bible for yourself, the more you will learn about God's great love for all the people of the epicenter—and the more you will be inspired to love them too.

Strategy No. 2: Pray

"Be joyful in hope, patient in affliction, faithful in prayer." —Romans 12:12, NIV

As you become more knowledgeable about the people of the Muslim world, let me encourage you to begin praying faithfully and consistently for them, because this is what the Bible teaches us to do. Here are ten specific ideas you might use in praying for the people of the epicenter:

1. Praise God that He loves *all* the people of the world and sent His Son to rescue *anyone* who will repent and turn to Him for salvation. (John 3:16)

2. Pray for the peace of Jerusalem and for the peace of all the people in the region. (Psalm 122:6)

3. Pray for God's blessing on Israel and her neighbors. (Genesis 12:1-3)

4. Pray for open doors for the gospel so that everyone in the epicenter can hear and respond to Christ's offer of salvation to anyone who believes. (Colossians 4:2-6; Revelation 3:20)

5. Pray for Christ-followers in the epicenter to have the courage to "fearlessly make known the mystery of the gospel" despite intense persecution that may accelerate in the years ahead. (Ephesians 6:19, NIV)

6. Pray for the Radicals and those who persecute the Church, that God would change their hearts and draw them into His Kingdom. (Matthew 5:44)

7. Pray that the Lord would open the hearts of the Christ-followers in the region so that they might know Christ even more fully than they do now. (Ephesians 2:15-23)

8. Pray that the Lord of the harvest would raise up and send out more laborers

because "the harvest" of souls "is plentiful." (Luke 10:2)

9. Pray without ceasing, and do so with thanksgiving, "for this is God's will for you in Christ Jesus." (1 Thessalonians 5:16-18)

10. Pray in the name of Jesus, for this is where the real power lies. (Matthew 18:19-20)

For more information on how to pray knowledgeably and consistently, you may want to sign up for my Flash Traffic e-mails at www.joelrosenberg.com.

Strategy No. 3: Give

"Do not store up for yourselves treasures on earth, where moth and rust destroy, and where thieves break in and steal. But store up for yourselves treasures in heaven . . . for where your treasure is, there your heart will be also." —Matthew 6:19-21

Once you begin to understand God's plan and purpose for the people of the epicenter and become devoted to prayer, please consider investing your time, your talents, and your treasure in the work God is doing in the Middle East, as the Scriptures command.

The people of the Middle East lack sufficient resources to meet their physical and spiritual needs, and by contributing to humanitarian organizations, you help provide relief supplies, training, and literature that shares the gospel. One such organization is the Joshua Fund, whose aim is to bless the people of the Middle East. You can learn more at www.joshuafund.net or by writing to:

The Joshua Fund
1890 Base Camp Road
Monument, CO 80132-8009

Strategy No. 4: Go

"Go therefore and make disciples of all the nations, baptizing them in the name of the Father and the Son and the Holy Spirit, teaching them to observe all that I commanded you; and lo, I am with you always, even to the end of the age."
—Matthew 28:19-20

Learning, praying, and giving are biblical responses, but they are not enough. To truly obey the teachings of the Bible and follow the model Jesus set for us, we need to be willing to turn off our TVs, get up off the couch, put away our iPods, and go love Muslims in the name of Jesus in real and practical ways.

I asked an MBB friend to list ten practical ways readers of this book can show the love of Jesus Christ to their Muslim neighbors.

Before you approach your Muslim neighbors, pray that the Holy Spirit would show you ways you might be able to love them the way Christ Himself would love them. Of course the Holy Spirit is the expert in this matter, but here are my suggestions.

1. Take your Muslim neighbor a "welcome to the neighborhood" gift, like a box of homemade cookies, a basket of fruits, chocolate, a card, a plant, or just flowers. If you are invited to their home, never go empty-handed.

2. Invite your Muslim neighbors to your home for dinner. As you invite them, ask them what they would like to eat. Make sure they understand that you are sensitive to their diet (no pork or alcohol).

3. When they come to your home, be very respectful. They may take off their shoes when they enter your home, as it is a tradition. You may ask them to keep their shoes on or you may take off your shoes as well.

(On the other hand, when you enter their home, please always take off your shoes.) Then, offer them a nonalcoholic drink. Out of respect, refrain from drinking alcoholic beverages in front of them. When seating them at the dinner table, if possible seat them at the head of the table away from the door or any entrance.

4. At dinner, pray for your new friends individually. Pray for the couple, their children, or whatever situation they may be in. And don't be afraid to pray in the name of Jesus.

5. At dinner, get to know your new Muslim friends. Ask about their culture, traditions, food, interests, etc. It is fun to learn about other cultures. Ask if you could meet again another time for coffee or tea and to continue building the friendship.

6. When you meet with them for coffee or tea, offer to pray for them individually regarding whatever is on their hearts.

7. Invite them to spend time with you and your Christian friends doing something fun and "safe"—that is, nonthreatening to their faith—so that they can see the love of Christ in His followers. This is very

attractive to Muslims. Eventually, you may want to ask them to a church function, like a Christmas or Easter service.

8. When you make dinner for your own family, consider making extra and taking some to your Muslim neighbor. Middle Easterners really appreciate this gesture. Again, no pork, please!

9. When any member of their family is ill, pray for that person with your Muslim neighbor. Take them chicken soup. Offer to do chores, like picking things up for them at the grocery store or the pharmacy. Offer to babysit if they need to go to a doctor's appointment, or—if you have time—offer to drive them to their appointment. Or just offer to babysit their kids so that the couple can have a date night.

10. If you go on vacation, bring back a souvenir for your neighbor. In the Middle East, that is very much appreciated. Remember their birthdays, and surprise them with a card, a gift, a cake, or flowers. In all things, follow the teachings of Jesus to "do to others as you would have them do to you" (Luke 6:31, NIV).

Loving your Muslim neighbor is the right way to begin, but we should not stop there. Jesus teaches us to "go" and make disciples of "all the nations." Keep in mind that the Lord may be calling you to serve Him in the Muslim world through short-term missions or full-time ministry. That may seem scary at first. But if it is God's will for your life, there can be no greater joy than obeying Christ's call. Seek wise counsel from pastors, ministry leaders, and friends who know you and who have experience doing ministry in cross-cultural environments, particularly in the Muslim world. Get as much training as you possibly can. Build a team of friends and allies who will pray faithfully for you and support you financially. Whatever you do, don't be a "lone ranger" and head into the Muslim world by yourself. Such an approach is neither biblical nor wise.

JESUS IS WITH US

Jesus tells us not to be afraid to serve Him. He promises to always be with us. He promises never to forsake us. Perhaps we should take Him at His word.

ENDNOTES

THE BIG, UNTOLD STORY

1. Author interview with an Iranian Christian leader on the condition of anonymity in 2007.
2. Patrick Johnstone et al, Operation World (Waynesboro: Authentic Media, 2001), p. 353.
3. Author interview with an Iranian Christian leader on the condition of anonymity in 2007.
4. Author interview with an Iranian pastor on the condition of anonymity in 2007.
5. Author interviews with Egyptian pastors and ministry leaders beginning in 2005 and continuing through the fall of 2008.
6. Author interview with a Sudanese evangelical leader, name and date withheld.
7. Author interviews with numerous Sudanese Christian leaders in 2008.

8. Author interview with an Arab pastor, name and date of interview withheld.

9. "Algeria bans Muslims from learning about Christianity," www.ArabicNews.com, March 21, 2006.

10. Interviews with Iraqi and Jordanian Christian leaders in 2008.

11. Author interview with Iraqi evangelical leader, name and date withheld.

12. Interviews with several senior Jordanian Christian leaders on the condition of anonymity in 2008.

13. The story was relayed to me by an Arab ministry leader who has interacted with this woman personally; name and date of interview withheld.

AIR WAR, GROUND WAR

1. Cited by Raymond Ibrahim, "Islam's 'Public Enemy #1,'" National Review, March 25, 2008.

2. Hormoz Shariat, interview with the author, January 2007.

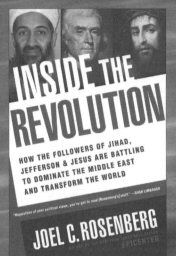